Winter Songbook

Seasonal Verses, Poems and Songs
for Children, Parents and Teachers

An Anthology for Family, School, Festivals and Fun!

Sally Schweizer

Sophia Books

Sophia Books
An imprint of Rudolf Steiner Press
Hillside House, The Square
Forest Row, RH18 5ES

www.rudolfsteinerpress.com

First published in 2018

© Sally Schweizer 2018

I have done my utmost to find authors and composers of all verses and songs. Most are out of copyright. I have been unable to trace some. If I have included something that is still in copyright, I apologise and would be grateful if the publisher, author or composer would get in touch so that I can request permission to include it in a further edition. (S.S.)

Benjamin Britten: Missa Brevis in D, Benedictus (excerpt) ©1959 by Boosey & Co Limited. Reproduced by permission of Boosey & Hawkes Music Publishers Ltd. Benjamin Britten: War Requiem, Benedictus (excerpt) ©1961 by Boosey & Hawkes Music Publishers Ltd.

Credits: extra photography; Bonnie Kittle, Aditya Saxena, Sandra Frey, Siarhei Plashchynski

A CIP catalogue record for this book is available from the British Library

ISBN 978 1 85584 552 7

Designed and typeset by yellowfish.design
Printed and bound by 4Edge Ltd., Essex

In memory of my husband, Christian,
and to my children, grandchildren and
all children, old and young, everywhere.

CONTENTS

CHAPTER 3. *Wintry Weather*

CHAPTER 4. *Winter Outdoors*

Appendix:

ACKNOWLEDGEMENTS

I am so grateful to:

The many children who have enjoyed everything from this anthology with me for so many years, thereby making them tried, tested and worthwhile publishing.

The many students, teachers and parents who have enjoyed songs, rounds, verses and circle times from my collections and those who asked when I was going to publish them.

My editor and publisher Sevak Gulbekian for his faith in me by asking if I had anything else for him to publish.

My son Mark Lange, who gave a huge amount of his time in helping me write all the music on the computer in my home in England and his home in Lisbon via 'clouds'. Extraordinary, the wonders of new science! Some music had been in my notebooks, some in my memory.

Howard Moody – inspired composer, conductor and keyboard player – for his Preface.

Mark Lange, Christine-Fynes Clinton and Howard Moody for helpful comments on the Introduction.

Janni Nicol for her friendship and support.

And of course to all the authors and composers who inspired me to use their creations in my collections.

For Photographs: friends and family; staff and parents of the St Michael Steiner School, Hounslow, London; Siletz Tribal Community, Oregon, USA; and Mrs Bridget Kitley for her mother, Enid Slater.

Michael Wirz for Nora Ward's poems.

The Holst Foundation for Imogen Holst's translation of 'Quem Pastores'.

Dr Nicholas Clark, Librarian, Britten-Pears Foundation, Aldeburgh, Suffolk, for his advice and support.

Mike Williams, Boosey and Hawkes, London, for help with copyrights for my uncle's works.

PREFACE

Sally's kindergarten was an inspiration for both children and parents – a haven of creativity that defied the trends of mainstream schooling. Walks, expeditions, puppet shows in the woods and bread ovens replaced textbooks and computers. The children were always on the move within a structured rhythm of activities, learning through their senses and experience rather than through abstract thought and competition.

Every morning the children would enter the space where atmosphere, reverence and respect were at the core of all activities. A seasonal nature table linked the rhythm of their learning to the greater changes of the seasons and play was focused on the refashioning of natural materials into new forms, both physically and imaginatively. The children were encouraged to 'wonder', to ask questions and be generally curious. Their musical rituals always felt part of the bigger rituals of the natural world, inspiring a respect for humanity, for nature, for being together.

During parents' evenings we were given the same creative tasks that our children had experienced during the day, immediately binding us together through 'doing' and understanding rather than instruction and reports. At the time it all seemed magical – it was – but of course behind it all was years of very conscious thought, experience and preparation that Sally shared with us by example. Here is her courageous attempt to articulate something of that journey, offering us a precious tool kit of ideas to be absorbed and made our own.

For me Sally's kindergarten was a true reflection of a free creative world. Music and the arts lay at the core of this. As a musical family, you can imagine the surprise one day as our daughter came home singing melodic fragments from Benjamin Britten's operas. Sally later admitted to being his niece, and described her own sense of gratitude for the extraordinary creative experiences she had received as a child, living around her uncle and experiencing the international coming together of musicians that he facilitated, as well as having the opportunity to perform in his legendary community opera *Noye's Fludde*. Sally's mission is to share something of her experience by putting stories, singing, music and movement (in other words 'opera') at the heart of children's experience.

Class 'performances' involved a simple circle in which the children faced each other to share epic sequences of music, simple action and poetry in many different languages. The children hadn't yet been formally taught to read or write, but they knew every word effortlessly through their instinct and memory and could engage with their whole being – the way that cultures have always shared stories and songs through the generations. Of course for some, this was not their favourite activity, but they were allowed to come in and out of the action without judgement. It

was the non-competitive togetherness that was so precious. The parents were always allowed in when everything was ready. We would surround the children creating an outer circle. There were no lead characters or front seats to aid the adoration of eager parents, but rather an atmosphere in which we could all participate in our own way in the profundity of simple stories and songs that the children would never forget.

Britten and Sally, early 1943 at the Old Mill in Snape, Suffolk.

Sally took on the responsibility to create material that would enchant and inspire the children. I now see the power of what she gave them – an aesthetic awareness of beauty and the arts that gave them a rich inner core of creativity, which would never leave them. Many years later, there seems to be an even more urgent need for people to recognise and appreciate the vital essence of this approach to early childhood and how it can shape and inspire compassionate minds for the future.

I know that her writing will continue to inspire future generations. Thank you Sally!

Howard Moody
May 2017

INTRODUCTION

'The most effective kind of education is that a child should play amongst lovely things.' – Plato

Play surely embraces music and language.

Birds sing, leaves rustle, play bricks fall down, dogs bark, Grandad hums out of tune, rain patters: this is all music.

Little children find their way into language and give us heavenly moments. This is all poetry.

Live song and rhyme have been at the heart of my existence from even before birth, as my mother sang to my brother. Throughout childhood I learnt songs and poetry: incidentally in the first years, later as exercise. I gathered the joy of other languages along the way into adulthood. With my children I sang and recited nursery and other rhymes, mainly in English but also other tongues. They didn't always understand the words but they loved their sounds. Three of their favourite bedtime songs were in German, Russian and Swiss German.

Yet no one needs to know a foreign language to sing to a child! Some readers speak another tongue anyway, another kind of music. Singing from the heart in whatever fashion is what's best.

One day I found some small books in seasonal colours, the perfect place to write the collection of all I had enjoyed for so long. Many teachers and students asked when I was going to publish them. So I hope you will enjoy them and enrich your own collections. There are wonderful anthologies from which I have drawn which will never go out of date, and I am grateful to many people for what they have given me. I owe a great deal to my musical heritage, particularly through my close relationships with my uncle, the composer Benjamin Britten, my two godfathers Uncle Robert (Britten), a fine musician, and Peter Pears, a wonderful tenor, and also my piano teacher, Imogen Holst (Gustav's daughter). My uncle dedicated his glorious children's opera *Noye's Fludde* to my siblings and me; I played violin in the first performances.

Yet no one needs to know a famous musician to sing to a child! Singing or speaking a rhyme can express one's feelings: happy, sad, excited, lazy, joyful or playful, treasured in the child's memory forever.

On the old Bridge by Snape Maltings, Suffolk, early 1943
l-r Myself rather invisible in pram, my mother Beth, my brother Sebastian, Peter Pears, Benjamin Britten.

11

Understanding through physical expression

Mime is an art conveyed by clowns who are not simply playing the fool but articulating life itself. Babies understand body language before that of the tongue; young children understand how we feel in what we do and how we do it. One's behaviour and mannerisms speak volumes, not least facial expressions. We often don't need words: just a gesture will show what we intend or how we feel. So when we sing or speak a rhyme, children's comprehension is enhanced by accompanying actions. Children with special needs also respond well to poetry and song with movement. Opportunity to act in this way according to their ability can be very helpful to them. Those in wheelchairs can enjoy singing and moving just as much. Children reciting, moving and singing can give the observant adult indication of something unusual, the child maybe needing some particular help or care. Life for many children is not helped by screentime, much noise, directed activity and little space or time to move or play freely. Even very young children have their own laptops and iPads with caricature song and movement. A mother told me recently her four-year-old had just been to her new school's disco arranged by parents, and it was too loud. Her daughter loves dancing but 'Why does it have to be so loud? It was painful. It must damage their ears.'

Our body is the most perfect and expressive instrument. Demonstrating wonderful things is magic for the child.

Incorporating movement and gesture

Many readers will be used to moving to music and verse. Using variety and contrasts is fun: humour and seriousness, **LARGE** and small, **loud** and soft, *fast* and s l o w. Some rhymes lend themselves to obvious actions, such as wandering about in the verse 'Old John Muddlecomb', wriggling in 'The Tadpole' (Spring collection) or being droopy and miserable in 'Drip, Drip, Drip'. Rocking enchants the baby in a lullaby. When walking, one can sing or speak in time to one's steps. Singing games, skipping and ball rhymes depend on moving. It all helps the brain to develop. I have written on this and other related subjects in my books, *Well, I Wonder* and *Under the Sky*.

Many rhymes and songs create a mood: stillness, humour, busyness. Growing up is never easy, and some children have a particularly challenging, unstable background, so moods of joy and happiness can be wonderful for them, a soothing and stabilizing break from reality. Repetition is not only beloved by the young but gives a feeling of security, especially to such challenged children. I believe it is better to repeat the same actions in rhymes and games to reinforce the meaning, rather than confuse them. No one would ever think of doing 'This Little Piggy Went to Market' differently! Fast rhymes followed by slow, calm ones can help fidgety, restless children. Coordination is generally not advanced enough for those under six to move hands and arms individually against each other, so it is better to use them together.

Apart from well known actions in some rhymes, I have made suggestions for others, but it is really good if you make up your own. You can turn many songs and rhymes into finger games, action poems or ring games. Lists in the Appendix may help expand your ideas. One action I made up was for everyone in a circle to lay their arms over their neighbour's shoulders, demonstrating a feeling of togetherness and love for each other. This can be helpful where there are those of different cultures together.

There is no end to what you can make up, from a half-hidden sun to a wriggly worm or lost ducklings. Let your imagination fly!

Make up your own words too!

There is little more exciting or lovely for children than an adult making up a rhyme for them. Whether ever so silly or really beautiful, it is special. If you have not yet tried it, please have a go. Children enjoy doggerel too. Some of mine is in the Summer collection under 'Silly Verses'. I have suggestions for rhyming words in the appendix but there are many more.

Is not the child's favourite story often the one you made up, or the one about when you were little?

Creating security, safety and calmness through singing or chanting.

'Music, ho! Music such as charmeth sleep!' – Titania, *A Midsummer Night's Dream*, Shakespeare

Singing to a restless, sleepless or crying child can have a magical effect, even the newborn. We know about rubbing a sore knee with a hug and little rhyme. Talking or singing in a chant can have a soothing effect or even make the child laugh the tears away: '<u>Once</u> u /<u>pon</u> a /<u>time</u> there /<u>was</u> a /<u>ve</u>-ry /<u>poor</u>-ly /<u>knee</u>'. Likewise, getting children to do things or to hurry up may be helped with a funny little chant rather than admonition. If the child doesn't want to go to bed: 'Oh where, oh where has your dressing gown / bed / the bath / toothbrush gone? Oh where, oh where can it be?' (derived from the nursery rhyme 'Oh where, oh where has my little dog gone?'). Children love silly things and it might just work. It doesn't need to make sense, in a way the sillier the better. A rowdy playtime can be transformed with a comical song. Trying to hurry the children to get dressed after swimming: 'Put on your shoes and then the socks; don't get dry or you'll not be wet.'

Most children do have a great sense of humour!

Music is the most social of the arts; the human voice is the greatest instrument of all

Children need to hear beautiful language along with simple and lovely music. Do sing along while making tea or the beds, when in the car or out with the buggy! Digital music and YouTube can be helpful for adults to learn a song for themselves, but they are no substitute to the child for the real person. *Nothing* beats the sound of the human voice.

You can find some of the songs here on the internet to help you; however, they are often accompanied by unnecessary syncopated (off the beat) rhythms, so just ignore that and listen to the tune. Children tend to move in an inharmonious, even aggressive way to jerky, syncopated music.

The tunes are generally not written in particular keys, with the exception of my uncle's music. Some may be too high or some too low: sing them wherever you feel comfortable, including my uncle's, if you can't find the beginning note.

If you are self-conscious, take heart: whatever you do seems miraculous for the child.

Music affects body and soul: musical and linguistic environment

Music can make us tremble or clasp our hands, dance for joy or weep. There is an increasing amount of noise today, so it is lovely to hear someone taking time to sing or say a rhyme. I believe babyish and caricature language is not very respectful. Constant music at home and in shops, including 'classical', is not helpful. Silence is ok! It is lovely if people restrain themselves from making phone calls or checking texts whilst pushing the buggy: preferably a person-facing one as children need to hear but also watch people speaking so they can learn themselves. Language is becoming increasingly abbreviated in social media so it is excellent for children to experience as good and clear language as possible. Speech, thoughts and pictures on various media often flit from one idea to another rather fast. The young child needs time to understand.

Children really enjoy a moment of suspense. You can bring this into many rhymes as a tiny antidote to the get-everything-now-rush-rush culture of today. For example, in 'Five Fat Peas' (Summer collection), the child or children will stay absolutely still, maybe quivering with excitement, while they wait for you to do 'popped!' In the rhyme 'Exercises', (also Summer collection) the child or group just loves to see what Baby Small will do next, and wait happily until 'he' or 'she' (your little finger/s) appear from hiding behind your or the child's ear, instead of doing it 'properly'.

If an adult takes a stick or two on a walk to play the 'flute', 'violin' or 'guitar' to a song or just 'la, la, la', children will join in because it is special and magical.

My brother reading to me.

My son reading to himself.

Once upon a time there seemed more time, but children still enjoy looking at books and pictures, and for the very young, again, again and again!

Repetition

'First, rehearse your song by rote,
To each word a warbling note.
Hand in hand with fairy grace
Will we sing and bless this place.'
– Titania, *A Midsummer Night's Dream*, Shakespeare

We know how babies and children love the same old things. This is the best basis for learning; repetition is great for memory building. If you repeat something often enough, you will likely learn it by heart yourself.

Once I told the children at kindergarten that I had just written a new play for them and was trying to learn it. Jamie, 6, said 'Don't worry. We'll help. You only have to do it with us once and then we'll know it and can tell you when you go wrong.'

Rhythm and beat

The unborn child hears in the womb. So it is wonderful if mothers sing! The first rhythm a baby is likely to hear is three beats in a bar: the swinging, rocking of the lullaby: 3/8 or 6/8. Skipping or galloping are also in three time: 3/8 or 3/4. Depending on the tempo (speed), the simple beat of 2/4 and 4/4 can be slow and reverent or conversely quick and down-to-earth, for instance trotting in 2/4 and marching in 4/4. When crowds get together and chant, it is typically in 4/4 time. '/Why /are we /wai/ting?' or '/What do we /want? A /decent /wage!' – '/When do we / want it? /Now!' (See note on p.33.)

People talk to babies in a naturally sing-song way. 'How are /You, my /Dar-/Ling,/ Have you just /Wo-ken /Up?' Bouncing a child on the knee is fun for both! 'This is the /way the /gentlemen /ride...'

All over the world, children love to dance, twirling around, leaping, stamping and clapping, moved by melody and rhythm. I found young children prefer to go round the circle clockwise, always in the same direction, except of course at the maypole as the ribbons have to be untied!

Is not necessary to understand about beat to make music with children! And please don't worry about not singing in tune or keeping to the rhythm. Of course it is better if both work but the main thing is that it is real and alive, and so much more valuable when you do it yourself.

The pentatonic scale

This is a traditional mode used all over the world in folk music, found on the piano's black keys, but it can begin on any note. With such notes mixed together, the music is always harmonious. 'Sail bonny boat, like a bird on the wing, over the sea to Skye', is typical. Children sing easily in this style. 'I'm the king of the castle, get down you dirty rascal', is a pentatonic chant. Children also sing happily in fifths (notes five apart, like 'Twinkle twinkle'). You can sing tunes on two notes, even on one, to convey particular moods. (See note regarding fifths on p.33.)

Foreign languages

It is lovely for children to hear the 'music' of other tongues, especially when they have classmates, carers and neighbours from other parts of the world. You can ask parents to teach you something from their own country to bring to class, or they may come themselves. It is really good to sing or speak them as well as possible. If English is not your mother tongue, you can share your heritage with others. On the whole I prefer original English material rather than translations as we have such a rich source to draw from. Translating is not always successful in rhyme, partly because the metre or beat are different, but it is not easy to convey the meaning in poetry, which is what rhyming and beat are also about.

Parents and carers singing at nursery or school

There are a number of rounds (canons) in my anthology as simple repetitive songs. However, they are also there for older children or adults with or without children. One person or group begins, then others follow one by one to make a wonderful sound. 'Oh I can't sing, I'll just listen!' Yet so long as there are two or three people who are fairly secure, everyone can join in without worrying. You can ask friends or colleagues to help if you are not sure.

I ended parents' evenings with a simple canon, also to sing around the children at the next celebration. Children love the swelling then dwindling sound around them. People relax. Marvellous!

Single parts or not? Sharing and an inclusive kind of storytelling

Singing games start with a groom, sad girl, prince, farmer, whoever, in the centre. Some children are quick to offer; others feel exposed. I let the children choose: 'I wonder who would like to be Poor Jenny' or 'Whoever wants to be the farmer can go in the middle'. Several might happily take that part all at once and I let them! It might end up a bit of a muddle but who cares, you carry on anyway! You could do this at a party, or the birthday child could take a few friends into the centre to begin. In kindergarten I knew who would respond to encouragement and did so where appropriate, but never made children come in against their will. I didn't have single parts in the little plays we did either: we just did the story all together in a ring, playing, singing and moving every role, so we all learnt everything. There is plenty of time for children to learn individual parts later. Those of six going on seven never questioned it.

Creating courage through music

Through an unfortunate set of circumstances, not of my doing, I was coming down a Swiss mountain one October afternoon, alone with my three children and four months' pregnant. I had been told to take the short cut down but didn't find it. No mobile phones then! To go back up and find another way was unthinkable. The small path we were on through woods with slippery long, dry grass down the steep slopes either side became narrower and narrower until it ceased to exist. Now it was getting dark. My five-year-old walked ahead, I held my four-year-old by the hand, put my two-year-old on my shoulders and felt my baby wriggling. I sang and the children joined in. We came into a meadow and could barely see, so bumped into things. First we sang a 'bumping into

boulders' song. We trod in cow pats so we sang a 'treading in cow pats' song. We walked into an electric fence so we sang an 'electric fence' song. I knew that there was a steep precipice to the valley below on our right and was of course frightened but it was essential to keep a semblance of calm and un-worry. Through singing and making up funny verses the children were not concerned although they were getting tired. Eventually I could see a wood ahead and, thinking 'nothing is too difficult for the brave', I thought I could keep us all warm enough, snuggled together, over and under piles of twigs and branches. Just then, the full moon appeared through the trees. Filled with happiness we sang our beloved moon song (see Autumn collection) which we had sung so often on our walks home in the dark from shopping:

> I see the moon and the moon sees me,
> I see the moon and the moon sees me,
> I see the moon and the moon sees me,
> I love the moon and the moon loves me.

As we entered the wood, we saw a little light from a hut in the distance. We found the track and made our way down, meeting the search party at the bottom. And I thanked heaven for the gift of music and the joy of singing.

> 'Through the house give glimmering light
> By the dead and drowsy fire;
> Every elf and fairy sprite
> Hop as light as bird from brier;
> And this ditty after me
> Sing and dance it trippingly.'
>
> – Oberon, *A Midsummer Night's Dream*, Shakespeare

CHAPTER 1

Christmas

At the kindergarten Whitsun festival, about which you may find notes in the Spring Collection, we sang songs from around the world in recognition of the different nationalities and cultures in the class at the time. We did the same at Christmas, because is this not truly the festival of children everywhere – whether Christian or not, commercial or not? As with all songs and verses in other languages I just told the children what they were about, rather than translate. That way they could immerse themselves in the music of the language as well as the actual words which were made clear by the accompanying actions. Through imitation and repetition they learnt them well and told their parents they could speak French, German, Italian or whatever!

I frequently had a student with a different mother tongue, and as part of their training they had to tell a story for the usual week and create a ringtime for the 3 or 4 weeks. I asked them to tell the story in their own language, as this was a true picture for these young children who were only embarking on their own language, rather than hear it with a foreign accent.

Silhouette: paper tree cut with tiny scissors by a friend.

(This was different for students with a regional dialect of course as it was their mother tongue.) A few words at the beginning of the story of what it was about was enough and the children sat happily listening to the 'music'. At ringtime the student would bring some English for their own sake, as they did have to learn it well, and some in their own tongue with their particular cultural gestures, as for instance beautiful Japanese.

I trust the songs and rhymes in foreign tongues that we did became a basis for their wanting to learn others and be open to different peoples. It may well be that you, dear reader, have a different mother tongue from English, and I hope that if you are a parent, carer, teacher or early years' practitioner, you also do your own songs and poems. This is a wonderful gift to share: please don't shy away from it!

For our Christmas play, parents, carers and various friends and relations sang some of the songs and carols with us. Much music was woven throughout, including the children's 'orchestra' mentioned in the Introduction: at Christmas just with metal instruments for a starry, twinkly, heavenly sound. We also used small seven-string pentatonic lyres which anyone can play by simply drawing their fingers across, or very gently plucking. We played these throughout the year. At festivals I sometimes offered (smilingly, thrust…!) them into the

hands of parents: they all knew we played them and some were happy, but others mouthed: 'I can't play this!' I would whisper sweetly, 'Yes you can! Just copy me!' So they did, and it was wonderful because it was easy and whatever you do together in the pentatonic is beautiful. You can find sources on the internet under 'Seven-stringed lyre'. Any instrument played to or with children is wonderful. I believe that there is truly a great difference between live and recorded music, including 'classical'.

Some like to celebrate Advent, the four weeks of 'waiting for' the Christchild's birth, with songs and a gradual making of decorations. This can be a lovely time for children to build up slowly, leaving a space away from the bustle of shopping and commercialism. Christmas Eve is the time for celebration in many countries. We did this too in my own family, and our tradition on Christmas day was to go off for a picnic, come rain or shine. The children were allowed to choose whatever yummy food they could find in the house. (I popped a few apples and such like in as well.) Various traditions about bringing light and joy into the darkness of winter hold fast around the world around this time, such as the Festival of Santa Lucia on 13th December in Sweden. I have never been to the Southern hemisphere, let alone in winter, so just have to imagine how Christmas might be, playing ball games on a sunny, warm beach with a decorated Christmas tree stuck into the sand. Saint Nicholas, the bringer of gifts, is celebrated around the world on the night of December 5th. A song for St Nicholas and a poem for Advent are to be found in my Autumn collection, as it is then not yet the winter solstice. Below are the songs and poems I used for one particular Christmas (ring-time) with a few notes in between. (I created every ringtime afresh: with a good collection to choose from, one meets the present children and one's work can never become stale.) On 6th January, twelve days after Christmas, we celebrated the coming of the Three Kings, the Festival of the Epiphany.

Expectant mums

We sang many carols at home and in class, too many to include here, and you will have your own particular favourites. Experiencing them live, however lovely they may sound when recorded, is - well – live – alive. Not for nothing do people want and advertise an event with 'LIVE BAND'. In these days of ubiquitous musack and background music in many homes, it is refreshing for the child to be surrounded by normal background noises and have peace from all recorded music. Children's ears are still developing and need protection, and many cannot properly listen any more as they have switched off internally. This is becoming ever more obvious already in nursery and primary schools. Young people are damaging their hearing with too loud music, also directly into the ear. Christmas is a time of Peace, and quiet. So what joy to sing 'Away

in a Manger' or other favourites again and again, at bedtime, at Auntie Joy's, in the park, over the wall at Mr Jones' down the road, going along the canal. There is even time to sing between the car park and the supermarket! Who cares! Lovely for others to hear and even join in! Be brave: *for is the child not more important than what people think?* There comes a time when it becomes embarrassing... But enjoy it while it lasts and carry on at home!

Benedictus

Blessed are those who come in the name of the Lord.

Latin Mass

Benjamin Britten
from 'Sanctus' in 'War Requiem'

Be - ne - di - ctus, be - ne - di - ctus   qui___ ve - nit in___ no-mi-ne

in___ no-mi-ne_____ Do-mi-ni,   in___ no-mi-ne_____ Do-mi-ni,

Benjamin Britten as a little child.

He did so much for music, for peace, for the disadvantaged and for children throughout the world in his short life, born November 22nd, Saint Cecilia's day (Patron Saint of Music) 1913 and died December 4th 1976.

Benedictus

from Missa Brevis in D

Benjamin Britten

Blessed are those who come in the name of the Lord.

MARY AND JOSEPH

Mary and Joseph had travelled far,
Tired were their steps, and slow.
Was it much further? They did not know,
Walking to Bethlehem.

Mary said softly, 'The night draws nigh,
Look at the starry sky.
We will find shelter by and by
When we reach Bethlehem'.

How Far is it to Bethlehem?

Francis Chesterton

1. How far is it to Beth - le - hem? Not ve - ry far. Shall we find the sta - ble room Lit by a star? 2.Can we see the lit - tle child, Is He with - in? If - we lift the wood - en latch May we go in?

3. May we stroke the crea - tures there, Ox, ass or sheep? May we peep like them and see Je - sus a - sleep? 4.If we touch His ti - ny hand, Will He a - wake? Will - He know we've come so far Just for His sake?

I did only these verses as the others are beyond the younger child. The rest are in the Oxford Book of Carols.

DEAREST MARY, COME INSIDE

Dearest Mary, come inside.
The kind innkeeper opens wide
The door of his warm stable.
There is no bed, no chair, no table,
But a manger for the little child,
And ox so strong and donkey mild.
Come, rest yourself on this soft, warm hay,
For in this haven we may surely stay.

Sally Schweizer

Given the opportunity and materials, children really enjoy making decorations and presents rather than buying them. I have come across those who think gifts are only valuable if bought because it means a financial 'sacrifice'. Yet the effort and love put into a hand-made gift cannot be replaced. It may be hard for busy parents to find the time to help, but many children can do wonderful things on their own, even if when they are still little they don't look like anything recognisable. Making simple straw stars is possible for quite young ones, or complicated as this for the older child. Instructions can be found in books or on the internet.

THE BIRTH OF JESUS, THE CHRIST CHILD

A wondrous sound steals through the night,
Like silver bells from distant height.
Like voices filled with joy and mirth,
Like stars alighting on the earth.

I have no 'proper' tune for this; we sang it on three notes.

Ai, Lyooli, Lyooli

Verses 1, 2, 3, & 4:

A - i lyoo - li, lyoo - li, A - i lyoo - li___ lyoo - li,

1. New - ly now born, My lit - tle - child.
2. How quiet - ly he sleeps, My lit - tle - child.
3. My sweet gol - den one, My lit - tle - child.
4. Beauti - ful, so good, My lit - tle - child.

АЙ ЛЮЛИ, ЛЮЛИ

Ай люли, люли, Ай люли, люли,
Новорожденный, Малютка мой.

Ай люли, и. т. д.
Как тихо он спит, Малютка мой.

Ай люли, и. т. д.
Золотой, невинный, Малютка мой.

Ай люли, и. т. д.
Красывый, хорошый, Малютка мой.

This is meant to be sung in Russian as there will be those among my readers who do speak it, but for others you will see the translation in the song which can be sung in not-very-brilliant English, if you like the tune! The third verse in Russian is 'My golden, innocent...' but it doesn't work at all really in English. You are of course free to do anything you like with this or anything I have written or composed, or not use them at all! Making up your own is always special, however simple.

My doctor congratulated me on the birth of my third child. I said modestly that it was the most natural thing in the world. 'WHAT!' he said. 'It is the greatest miracle of all!'

I made the cradle from layers of undyed sheepswool. They were laid crosswise and wrapped around a tennis ball: with a dyed pink layer first and a dyed blue layer last. Then I worked it with my hands using hot-as-possible water and soap flakes until felted. After rinsing, I cut a piece out to remove the ball and make space for the baby. Coloured sheep's wool was used for the baby and wrappings. If you enjoy handwork but are not familiar with this technique, you can find books on felting. There is a new and popular technique of using a needle with a barb to felt the wool, but I prefer the traditional, softer method.

My aunt, a health visitor, told me before my first child was born: 'Wrap baby up tight, like in the womb, then he or she will feel safe and well.'

Lully, Lullay

Coventry Carol

Lul - ly, lul - lay, thou lit - tle ti - ny child, Bye, bye, lul - ly, lul - lay. - Lul -

ly, lul - lay, thou lit - tle ti - ny child, Bye, bye, lul - ly, lul - lay.

Just the first verse of this wonderful carol is suitable for young children, the others for children over 8 or 9. Although it is in the minor key, it does not feel so, and children love it. The other verses can be found in carol books.

AWAY IN A MANGER

This gentle, much-loved little carol was written by a poet, possibly American, who truly understood the hearts of children. Just in case you don't know it, you will find the song on the internet.

We three were in the bath, asking where babies come from. 'What I should really like to know,' said my older brother of 6 (putting my mother in a momentary quandary as to how to explain more than 'from Mummy's tummy' in front of us two little girls), 'Is how they fit door handles onto doors.'

Ihr Klare Seraphim

Switzerland

1. Ihr kla - re Se - ra - phim, In das Stall gänd oi - e Schyn. O -
2. Do lyts im Chrip - pe - li, das fü - rig Härz - e - li. O -
3. I Schläch - ti Win - de - li, mues es y - bun - de sy. O
4. Bim Ochs und E - se - li lyts do im Chrip - pe - li. O -

Je - sus sal - ve! O Je - sus sal - ve.
Je - sus sal - ve! O Je - sus sal - ve.
Je - sus sal - ve! O Je - sus sal - ve.
Je - sus sal - ve! O grües - sed sChrist chind - li.

A Swiss carol *(rough translation)*

You bright angels
Shine your light into the stable!
Oh welcome, Jesus.
There he lies in the manger,
The fiery little heart,
He must be wrapped
In poor swaddling clothes.

A Little Child on the Earth Has Been Born

Flemish carol

1. A lit - tle child on the earth has been born, He came_____ to
2. He came to earth for the sake of us all, And wish - es us

earth for the sake of us all,
all_____ a hap - py new year.

27

Il Est Né, le Divin' Enfant

France

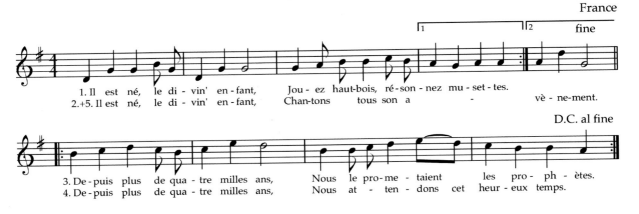

1. Il est né, le di - vin' en - fant, Jou - ez haut-bois, ré - son - nez mu - set - tes.
2.+5. Il est né, le di - vin' en - fant, Chan - tons tous son a - vè - ne-ment.

3. De - puis plus de qua - tre milles ans, Nous le pro - me - taient les pro - ph - ètes.
4. De - puis plus de qua - tre milles ans, Nous at - ten - dons cet heur - eux temps.

Joyful cello playing with wooden spoon
and invisible strings.

The given translation:

He is born, the Heavenly Child,
Oboes play; set bagpipes sounding
He is born, the Heavenly Child.
Let all sing His nativity.

'Tis four thousand years and more,
Prophets have foretold His coming,
'Tis four thousand years and more,
Have we waited this happy hour.

This old French carol, to be found in the *Oxford Book of Carols*, is a great favourite. In my kindergarten we would walk around singing with our make-believe instruments: 'trumpets', 'recorders', 'guitars', 'cellos', 'pianos', 'harps', 'violins', 'flutes', whatever the children wanted, just singing the original French. It is lovely to do this at home too. There are many more verses to be found on the internet.

Sometimes on a walk I picked up a stick or two and begin to 'play', copied by my children or those in my class, singing la-la-la to a happy tune. Some are familiar with an instrument. Many readers may play something or know someone who does. If you work with children, perhaps you can invite someone to visit who plays an instrument. It doesn't matter how modest it is, the main thing is that it is a living, real sound and children can watch how it is done. I hope our kindergarten 'orchestra' of percussion instruments sowed a seed for learning another instrument later on.

THE SHEPHERDS COME

WAKE UP SHEPHERDS

Wake up shepherds, hear us sing,
Listen to the news we bring:
A baby is born to you this night
Whose love will fill your hearts with light.

You'll find Him where ox and ass are stabled,
There in the manger He lies cradled.
So wake up shepherds, hear us sing,
Song Gloria to our new born king.

I don't know the author of this happy carol. It really does call for joyful music: I used one of my own tunes for it but make up your own or use another. Wooden or metal percussion instruments fit well.

Quem Pastores Laudavere
Shepherds Left Their Flocks A-Straying

English translation by Imogen Holst

Mediaeval

Quem pas - to - res lau - da - ve - re, Qui - bus an - ge - li, dix - e - re.
Shep - herds left their flocks a - stray - ing, God's - com - mand - with joy o - bey - ing,

Ab - sit vo - bum jam ti - me - re, Na - tus est - rex glo - ri - e.
When they heard the an - gels say - ing, Christ is born - in Beth - le - hem.

Translation

Run you shepherds, run all together.
Take reed-pipes and pipes with you.
Run all together, with a joyful sound
To Bethlehem to the manger, to the manger in the stable.

You can find more verses on the internet.

Such a lovely carol! With young children you can sing just the first verse, also in Latin: why not! To the little child it is no different from their own language or any other. Is music language or language music? Babies have the potential to speak any tongue. When parents joined us they sang all three verses, usually just in English! Adults' thinking can get in the way, whereas children just copy (which makes them so vulnerable generally).

My little twin granddaughters were used to having suncream spread over their skin. One of them sat at the supper table, put her hands into her white yoghurt and smeared it carefully over her arms.

Laufet Ihr Hirten
(Run, You Shepherds)

Germany

Lau-fet, ihr Hir-ten, lauft al - le zu - gleich. euch! Lauft al - le zu
Neh-met Schal - mei - en und Pfeif-fen mit

mal, mit freu-di-gem Schall, Nach Beth-le-hem zum Kripp-lein, zum Kripp-lein im Stall!

MARY ROCKS HER BABY

Mary rocks her baby,
Joseph holds a light,
Ox and ass are standing
In the stable bright.

Shepherds in the doorway
Come to greet the child,
Now they stand before Him
And His mother mild.

One holds out a lambkin,
Soft and white as snow.
All shall give their presents,
Ere they homeward go.

H. St John

30

This is the version (below, left) I have known for many years. However, in researching for copyrights, I came across this lovely one (right) which I assume is the original.

I SAID THE DONKEY

I said the donkey, all shaggy and brown,
I carried his mother to Bethlehem town.

I said the ox, all white and red,
I gave him some hay to pillow his head.

I said the lambkin, as white as snow,
I gave him some wool to cover his toe.

I said the spider, swinging down to the floor,
I wove him a web, to make him a door.

I said the dove, from the rafters high,
I cooed him to sleep so he would not cry.

I said the robin, all red aglow,
I fanned the flames to melt the snow.

Jesus our brother, kind and good
Was humbly born in a stable rude
And the friendly beasts around Him stood
Jesus our brother, kind and good.

"I," said the donkey, shaggy and brown,
"I carried His mother up hill and down;
I carried her safely to Bethlehem town."
"I," said the donkey, shaggy and brown.

"I," said the cow, all white and red
"I gave Him my manger for a bed;
I gave Him my hay to pillow His head."
"I," said the cow, all white and red.

"I," said the sheep with curly horn,
"I gave Him my wool for His blanket warm;
He wore my coat on Christmas morn."
"I," said the sheep with curly horn.

"I," said the dove from the rafters high,
"Cooed Him to sleep that He should not cry;
We cooed Him to sleep, my mate and I."
"I," said the dove from the rafters high.

"I," said the camel, yellow and black,
"Over the desert, upon my back,
I brought Him a gift in the Wise Men's pack."
"I," said the camel, yellow and black.

Thus every beast by some good spell
In the stable dark was glad to tell
Of the gift he gave Emmanuel,
The gift he gave Emmanuel.

Cyclamen in hoar frost

SLEEP, LAMBKIN, SLEEP

Sleep, lambkin, sleep,
Sleep upon the hill.
Oh good little lambkin sleep,
Sleep, lambkin, sleep.

Wake, lambkin, wake,
Wake upon the hill,
Oh good little lambkin wake,
Wake upon the hill.

Jump, lambkin, jump,
Jump upon the hill,
Oh good little lambkin jump,
Jump upon the hill.

Dance, lambkin, dance,
Your little bells now ring,
Oh good little lambkin dance,
Dance upon the hill.

I thought this was by Christina Rossetti but am unable to find it anywhere. She wrote many marvellous, inspired poems for children.

THERE WAS A LITTLE GARDEN

There was a little garden
Lay deep beneath the snow,
But Mary came a-walking
And found the Christmas rose.

There was a little thorny bush
Whose branches all were bare,
But Mary came a-walking
And found the robin there.

The sheep were on the hillside
All frozen on the ground,
But Mary came a-walking
And found the new-born lamb.

She wears the rose upon her head,
The robin in her hand,
And in her arms so gentle,
She bears the new-born lamb.

This is particularly lovely if sung to a simple, slow tune, with gentle hand and arm gestures. I have not put the one I used here specifically to encourage you to find or make up your own!

I am aware that what I say regarding particular music and related movement for young children may make me dated and old-fashioned. Yet I have enough experience of jerky, in harmonious rhythms bringing about ugly movements and gestures in children to make these suggestions. In older children it is not so important, yet up to 9 or 10 years old I really think it is better in the main to avoid it where possible. A friend told me his son of 7 joined a band with such music but soon left as it was 'awful'. His next son tried it later with the same result. In homes where there are older children, of course compromise must be found, but most apparatus also has a volume button! There are of course many exceptions where the tune with some syncopation does not give an ugly physical reaction, such as in folk music and the wonderful building song of my uncle's children's opera *Noye's Fludde*.

I hope readers will understand what I mean by 'swooping' up to the note rather than landing straight on it. For children it is best to make a clean landing rather than a bit of glissando! It also helps them to sing in tune. Men will find that children usually copy them naturally an octave (or even two) higher.

Interestingly, I have always found a particular affinity to the interval of a perfect fifth, long before I knew its musical and scientific significance. In my work with young children I began to see how easily they sing this interval (and even one fifth above another). My uncle often used it, for instance in Miles' Latin song, in his opera *The Turn of the Screw*, or the opening of the *Serenade for Tenor, Horn and Strings*. The children I taught loved the songs I made with these tunes. You can find the most marvellous and moving example of this interval in Thomas Tallis' 40-part motet *Speum in Allium*, written in 1570 for 8 choirs of 5 voices each.

Just after I wrote these last paragraphs, I joined a huge march in London, my first ever but for something I felt strongly about. It was very peaceful. Even the hundreds of police were smiling and happy. Every now and then, someone started a chant, and every single time it was in the classic 4/4 rhythm (see Introduction). People had brought saucepan lids, whistles and various other bangers and blowers. One couple had brought a drum each, tuned to a perfect fifth, which they played in different rhythms for 20 minutes or so, and it was never boring.

NEW YEAR

You may enjoy this great song for Epiphany with its old tune, 'Lilliburlero'.

An old tune: Lilliburlero

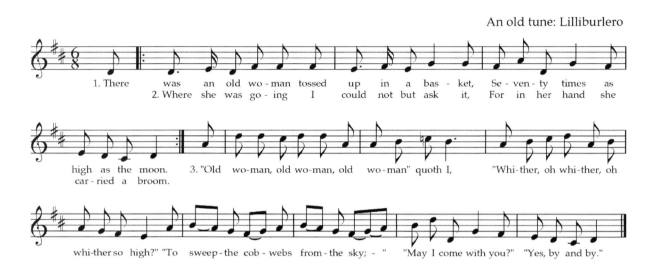

1. There was an old wo-man tossed up in a bas-ket, Se-ven-ty times as
2. Where she was go-ing I could not but ask it, For in her hand she

high as the moon. 3. "Old wo-man, old wo-man, old wo-man" quoth I, "Whi-ther, oh whi-ther, oh
car-ried a broom.

whi-ther so high?" "To sweep-the cob-webs from-the sky; - " "May I come with you?" "Yes, by and by."

There Was An Old Woman

This old song may refer to all manner of historical figures, not least Befana, the Italian woman who was so busy sweeping her house clean after meeting the three kings that she missed the birth of the Christ Child, and is forever traversing the heavens in search of Him. But she brings gifts to children on January 6th, as she says any of them might be the Christ Child, much as St Nicholas brings gifts on December 5th.

CHAPTER 2

Winter Indoors

I saw a stuffed toy like these, in the picture on the left, in a shop front in Sweden and made notes. I often made them as presents for children. They really love them. Crochet or knit a cup shape (or a tube which you gather at the bottom). Then make the hat: a cone shape starting at the top, increasing stitches at the brim. Fill the body and hat with sheepswool, stitch together, add a beard of fleece or sheepswool and a bead for a nose and hey presto! your old person comes alive!

I'm a Little Teapot

I'm a little teapot, short and stout,
Stand straight

Here's my handle, here's my spout.
Put one hand on hip, then the other hand kinked as a Z pointing down

When I see the teacups, hear me shout:
'Tip me up and pour me out!'
Tip body so 'spout' goes up and down

FINGER TWIST
No words! But you could make some up!

With your palms together, turn your middle fingers down past each other. Twist your hands, keeping the other fingers straight, still facing each other. Now you can wiggle the middle fingers: easy to do it the wrong way so it doesn't work!

BUBBLE, SAID THE KETTLE

Bubble, said the kettle, bubble, said the pot,
Bubble, bubble, bubble, we are very, very hot.
Shall I lift you from the fire? No, you needn't trouble:
That is just the way we talk: bubble, bubble, bubble.

This is very funny as an action poem.

JACK BE NIMBLE

Jack be nimble,
Jack be quick
Jack jump over the candlestick

JUMPING JOAN

Here am I,
Little jumping Joan
When no one is with me, I'm all alone.

Bubbles

KNOCK AT THE DOOR

Knock at the door. (*Knock on child's forehead*)
Pull the bell. (*Twitch a lock of hair*)
Look in the window. (*Lift eyelid*)
Lift the latch. (*Finger under nose*)
Walk in. (*Fingers 'walk' onto lips*)
Go down in the cellar. (*Run fingers down to tummy*)
And eat apples. (*Tickle tummy*)

SOMETIMES

Sometimes I'm very, very tall,
And sometimes I'm very, very small.
Close your eyes and turn around
And guess which I am now.

Joyful Jumping

Small and Tall

DIDDLE DIDDLE DUMPLING

Diddle diddle dumpling,
My son John
Went to bed with his trousers on.
One shoe off and one shoe on,
Diddle diddle dumpling,
My son John.

'My head is so long I couldn't fit in a shoebox' – a 5-year-old.
From where does such a fabulous image come?

Might 'Diddle diddle dumpling' help unwilling dressers? Children coming out of the swimming pool whose mothers are in a hurry, 'running a tight schedule', needing to 'get home quickly' or any number of urgent things, may not be responding to her needs or the threat of not getting any chocolate or dinner, or party next week either. Young children have little sense of time, and chiding does not usually help. Praise or something like this, which I made up on the spot, could catch their attention.

First your shoes and then your hat,
Quite easy to do if your shirt is flat.
Now your coat and then a sack,
Wonderful, a piggy back.

It doesn't even have to rhyme, and this is all rubbish, but such silliness might get the children's attention and encourage them to concentrate on the job in hand. I have often found making up something on the spur of the moment can be helpful. I am sure you can, or already do it too! Just be open to what you never thought you could do and ignore what other people think. They might love it!

Sometimes children in my kindergarten didn't want to get dressed in the morning at home. Many readers will be familiar with this! So I said to their parents in front of them that they could just bring them in their pyjamas (and I meant it). It worked like magic.

My Old Grandpa Clock

My old grand - pa clock goes tick, tock, tick, tock.

My old grand - ma clock goes tick, tock, tick, tock, tick, tock, tick, tock

But my lit - tle po - cket watch goes tick- a- tock- a, tick- a- tock- a, tick - a - tock - a tick.

IN A TINY LITTLE HOUSE

In a tiny little house, so very, very quiet,
so very, very small,
There lived three tiny mice, so very, very quiet,
so very, very small,
Nobody knew they were there at all –
When all of a sudden..........................(long pause)
...... OUT they popped!

Cup hands tightly round each other for the house, leaving a little hole in the thumbs to put the eye onto for peeping inside. Pop the thumbs and an index finger out. Children like to wait several seconds before popping out! How they love to imitate very tiny, squeezy things, followed by great big bold things. This is one of the rhymes I used as a picture of holding back, an antidote to the rushed and over stimulated environment with which many children live.

In my kindergarten at break-time, we lit a candle before saying grace. I lit the match (these were of course stored safely out of reach) and from it a wax taper. This I gave in silence to whichever child whose turn it was, from the youngest of three to the oldest of six plus. The littlest ones were helped by an adult. This child then carried the taper to the candle on a table, protecting the flame from blowing about by holding the hand a few centimetres behind it. It was also a nice gesture of caring for the fire. The child then lit the candle, blew out the taper and returned it to me. (In a conversation with a fire safety officer in 2017, I told him about this and how I thought it helped the children to have respect and care for fire. He thought it an excellent idea, and it is a pity that for health and safety reasons it is generally not allowed now.)

NINNY NANNY NETTICOAT

Ninny Nanny Netticoat
In a white petticoat,
The longer she stands
The shorter she grows.

Answer: a candle

Home-made wrought iron candle holder

FIVE FAT SAUSAGES
Five fat sausages,
Sizzling in the pan,
All of a sudden,
One went 'Bang'!

Four fat sausages,
Sizzling in the pan,
Et cetera

One fat sausage,
Sizzling in the pan,
All of a sudden,
It went 'Bang'!
No fat sausages,
Sizzling in the pan,
All of a sudden,
None went 'Bang'!

Little child with glorious tribal costume and moccasins at the Siletz Pow Wow, Oregon

Wiggle fingers, then clap at 'Bang'.
Of course in the last verse there will be no 'Bang!' !

This is good as a finger rhyme but also as an action poem with children wriggling, jumping and falling over, or just for baby's enjoyment at the 'bang's'!

Enjoying funny noises at 5-months-old

COBBLER, COBBLER

Cobbler, cobbler, mend my shoe,
Get it done by half past two.
Half past two is much too late,
Get it done by half past eight.

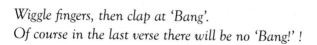

My great grandmother with my mother in the silk christening gown my grandmother made firstly for my aunt. My composer uncle wore the gown as well.

It can be seen at the Benjamin Britten exhibition at the Red House, Aldeburgh, Suffolk, together with the woollen cape.

HERE ARE GRANDMA'S GLASSES

Here are grandma's glasses, *Put hands round eyes*
Here is grandma's hat, *Make a 'hat' on the head*
Here are grandma's hands, *Show hands*
Folded in her lap. *Action obvious!*

A good way to help children sit still. You may like to repeat it with 'cap' instead of 'hat': I think the repetition works even better.

I AM A COBBLER

I am a cobbler, and this is what I do:
Tap-a-tap, tap-a-tap, to mend a shoe.
I am a cobbler, and this is what I do:
Stitch-a-stitch, stitch-a-stitch, to mend a shoe.
I am a cobbler, and this is what I do:
Stick-a-stick, stick-a-stick to mend a shoe.

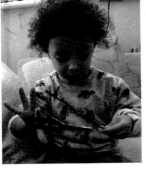

Given the opportunity, young children are quite capable already.

The girl stitching is making a hobby horse from an old sock.

I CAN TIE MY SHOELACES

I can tie my shoelaces, I can brush my hair,
I can wash my hands and face, and dry myself with care.
I can clean my teeth, and fasten up my frock.
I can say 'How do you do', and pull up both my socks!

Would anyone say 'frock' now? Does it matter? My class, neither boys nor girls, never commented, it was just fun to do a pretend zzzzziiiiiiiiiipppp or lightning quick buttons for the frock. All words are endlessly new and exciting!

Washing himself on holiday.

MISS POLLY HAD A DOLLY

Miss Polly had a dolly who was sick, sick, sick,
So she phoned for the doctor to be quick, quick, quick.
The doctor came with his bag and his hat
And he rapped at the door with a rat, tat, tat.
He looked at the dolly and he shook his head,
He said: Miss Polly, put her straight to bed.
He wrote on a paper for a pill, pill, pill,
I'll be back in the morning with my bill, bill, bill.

Accompany Miss Polly with claps, nods, jumps, steps and stamps to the beat. The music lies already in the words, but you can sing it if you want to on just two notes, one to each line or half line.

The naming ceremony of dolls made by the children of 4 to 6 virtually without instruction.

MIX A PANCAKE

Mix a pancake, stir a pancake,
Pop it in the pan.
Fry a pancake, toss a pancake,
Catch it if you can!

Christina Rossetti

Suitable for any time but of course especially on Shrove Tuesday.

Children like to cook and bake, with a little help to turn on the oven and get the hot cakes out.

MRS MASON

Mrs Mason broke a basin.
Mrs Mack heard it crack.
Mrs Frost asked how much it cost,
Half-a-crown, said Mrs Brown,
What a story, said Mrs Flory.

Children especially like to flap their hands at the last line.

Pat-a-Cake

Pat - a - cake, Pat - a - cake, Ba - ker's man, Bake me a cake - as fast as you can. Pat it and prick it and mark it with T, And there will be plen - ty for ba - by and me. For ba - by and me, for ba - by and me, And there will be plen - ty for ba - by and me.

An old rhyme to play on a baby's hand. Some say 'mark it with B'.

Lovely warm soapy water, clean rinsing water, clean cloth to dry up, cupboards to put it all in neatly: happy social, daily activity to share for the sake of everyone else.

SING A SONG OF WASHING UP
(to the tune of 'Sing a song of sixpence')

Sing a song of washing up,
Water hot as hot.
Cups and saucers, plates and spoons,
Dishes – such a lot.
Work the dishcloth round and round,
Wash them clean as clean,
Polish with a dry white cloth:
How busy we have been!

There were Ten in the Bed

1. There were ten in the bed, And the
3. So they all rolled over, And
4. So there were nine in the bed, And the

lit - tle one said, 2. Roll o - ver, Roll o - ver,
one fell out!
lit - tle one said, 5. Roll o - ver, Roll o - ver,

Continue with one falling out each time until:

So they all rolled over   *Or,*   So they all rolled over
And one fell out   *which is what we did:*   And one fell in
So there were none in the bed   So there were two in the bed
And the little one said   And the little one said
'Game over, game over'.   'Roll over, roll over' etc.

We did this in class with two 'beds' (2 rows) of children lying on the floor... they thought it hilarious.

Bye, Baby Bunting

Bye, Ba - by Bun - ting, Dad - dy's gone a - hun - ting,

Gone to get a rab - bit skin, to wrap a Ba - by Bun - ting in.

Repeat as long as you and baby wish!

CHAPTER 3

Wintry Weather

WINTER IS SNEEZY, BREEZY, FREEZY

Spring is flowery, showery, bowery,
Summer is hoppy, croppy, poppy,
Autumn is slippy, drippy, nippy,
Winter is sneezy, breezy, freezy.

A glorious phenomenon: hoar frost

Many moons ago when we were young, we had leggings to keep us cosy in winter. They had little buttons which we did up with button hooks, as did the shoes apart from lace-ups. It took a few minutes but I guess it added to our dexterity. Our coats had buttons rather than zips, an advantage in that they didn't get stuck, and it was good for little fingers. You can still find such clothes. Little hands keep warm in gloves which don't get lost when stitched to elastic threaded through the sleeves and round the back of the neck. There is something to be said for taking time to dress and undress, and doesn't it feel nice to be all wrapped up? At my local gym, some parents dress and undress their children even up to 6-years-old for the pool, and it is *definitely* not usually quicker!

A palette of snow

Plunging about in snowdrifts or just piles of snow is great fun. Many people take to the big snowy slopes in winter, yet whizzing down a little hill on a tea tray is also superb! When we had enough snow in kindergarten, we did just that, but when there was a bit more than enough, I took my old wooden skis there. We tramped up the rather little hill behind, and each child in turn had a ride down standing on the back of them. I was young enough then not to get too exhausted herring-boning back up the hill for several turns for each of the twenty-plus children. Of course they went home telling their parents they could ski!

Oh Where Do You Come From?

Germany

1. Oh where do you come from, You - lit - tle flakes of snow, Fal - ling
2. On the trees and on the bush - es, On the moun - tains a - far. Oh,

soft - ly, soft - ly fal - ling On the ear - th be - low?
tell me, do you come from Where the an - gels are?

As noted elsewhere, I tend to avoid translations, partly because we have so much beautiful language in English, but the song above is beautifully translated (I don't know by whom) and really speaks to children. It makes a lovely bedtime song. As far as I know, only the first verse is translated, the second is written by someone else. Here is the original:

SCHNEEFLÖCKCHEN, WEISSRÖCKCHEN

Schneeflöckchen, Weissröckchen,
Nun kommst du geschneit.
Du kommst aus den Wolken,
Dein Weg ist so weit.

Komm, setz' dich ans Fenster,
Du lieblicher Stern,
Mal Blumen und Blätter,
Wir haben dich gern.

Snow on the hillside

Crocheted snowflake

If you can crochet, you can make white snowflakes or angels or golden yellow stars. To hang up, simply immerse them in starch and iron them. If you make a cone-skirted angel, pop it over a cardboard cone to starch it. They are all a bit tricky to make but lovely for the children. You can find how to crochet, as well as many patterns, in books or in Pinterest on the internet.

LOOK OUT

Look out, look out, Jack Frost is about,
He' s after your fingers and toes,
And all through the night this gay little sprite
Is working where nobody knows.

He'll climb a tree, so nimble is he,
His silvery powder he'll shake.
To the window he'll creep, and while you're asleep,
Such wonderful pictures he'll make.

Across the grass he'll softly pass
And turn all the greenness to white.
Then home he will go, and laugh ho, ho, ho!
What fun I have had in the night!

In countries where the temperature drops below freezing, an advantage for those without double glazing (as in my childhood) is that children can wake in the morning to see what Jack has done on their window. He also enjoys 'painting' on car windows.

James wanted to take his very long icicle to bed with him. 'It will have to have a bath if it's going to bed with you,' said his mother.

THE SNOWMAN

We made a man all by ourselves
We made him jolly fat,
We stuffed a pipe into his face
And on his head a hat.
We made him stand upon one leg
That so he might not walk.
We made his mouth without a tongue
That so he might not talk.
We left him grinning on the lawn
That we to bed might go,
But in the night he ran away
And left a heap of snow.

NOW WINTER IS HERE

Now winter is here, with snow and with sleet,
The poor little birds have nothing to eat.
I give them some crumbs, they come with a rush,
The sparrow and robin, the wren and the thrush.
They come close beside me, their little hearts bold,
Their fear has all banished with hunger and cold.

IN THE WINTERTIME

In the winter time we go,
Walking in the fields of snow,
Where every bush and fence and tree
Is as white as white can be.

In the early spring we go,
When rain falls and winds still blow,
And every bush and fence and tree
Is as wet as wet can be.

In the showery spring we go,
When farmers plough and till and sow,
Where every bush and fence and tree
Is as soft as soft can be.

In the sunny spring we go,
When caterpillars waken and flowers grow,
Where every bush and fence and tree
Is filled with butterfly, bird and bee.

James Stephens

DOCTOR FOSTER

Doctor Foster went to Gloucester,
In a shower of rain,
He stepped in a puddle, right up to his middle,
And never went there again.

Very funny to do indoors but even funnier outside in wellies.

*The tit is so hungry it dares to land
on a finger for some crumbs.*

SNOWDROPS

I like to think
That, long ago
There fell to earth
Some flakes of snow
Which loved this cold,
Grey world of ours
So much, they stayed
As snowdrop flowers.

*Snowdrops eagerly pushing though brambles
in the early winter sunshine.*

The North Wind Doth Blow

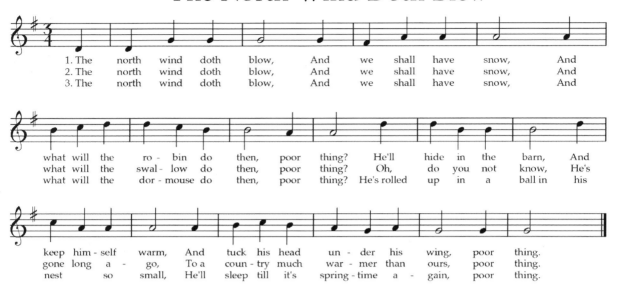

1. The north wind doth blow, And we shall have snow, And
what will the ro - bin do then, poor thing? He'll hide in the barn, And
keep him-self warm, And tuck his head un - der his wing, poor thing.

2. The north wind doth blow, And we shall have snow, And
what will the swal - low do then, poor thing? Oh, do you not know, He's
gone long a - go, To a coun - try much war - mer than ours, poor thing.

3. The north wind doth blow, And we shall have snow, And
what will the dor - mouse do then, poor thing? He's rolled up in a ball in his
nest so small, He'll sleep till it's spring - time a - gain, poor thing.

This and similar verses bring out the most loving, sweet aspects in children. They like to make small stroking and caressing gestures and curl up in a ball themselves, both boys and girls. Even the most challenging children can warm to such a verse.

THE SNOW FLAKES ARE WHIRLING

The snowflakes are whirling so fast and so light
To clothe our brown earth in a mantle of white.
See, down they come dancing, the fairy light things,
Like feathers let fall from an angel's wings.

The pine trees hang heavy, their branches are bowed,
Till they shake it all off in a fluffy white cloud;
It lies on the beds where the tiny flowers sleep
And everywhere's wrapped in a silence so deep.

You beautiful snow, how I wish you would stay,
But I know that tomorrow you'll vanish away.
The sunshine will come and you'll turn into rain –
0 promise me please that you'll soon come again.

Nora Ward

COLD WINTER'S IN THE WOOD

Cold winter's in the wood,
I'm sure I saw him pass,
Crinkling up the fallen leaves
Along the grass.

Dark winter's in the wood,
All the leaves have flown,
Leaving the poor cold trees
Shivering alone,

King winter's in the wood,
I'm sure I saw him go,
Crowned with a coronet
Of crystal snow.

Dark winter's in the wood,
All the trees are bare.
All the birds must fly away
To find their food elsewhere.

Eileen Matthias

Snow-laden trees on the Czech/Slovak border

Hoar frost on gorse.
'When the gorse is not in flower, kissing is not in season.'
(You can always find gorse out somewhere, even in
November.)

MARCH WIND

He huffs from the north,
He puffs from the south,
He bulges his cheeks
And purses his mouth.

His swagger is cloaked
In blue of the sky.
He wears a white cloud
Tipped over an eye.

He shakes the tall tree
Till stout branches ache.
He ruffles the river
And tramples the lake.

He's rough and he's bluff,
And his voice is a roar.
'Awake, lazy earth
Spring is coming once more.'

Maud Usholo

53

THE SILVER RAINDROPS PATTER

The silver raindrops patter
Upon the earth today.
Tip, tip, their knock is gentle
And this is what they say:
Oh little seeds awaken
And open wide your door,
Come out in pretty dresses
For spring is here once more.

DRIP, DRIP, DRIP

Drip, drip, drip, what a doleful sound,
Water pouring down from heaven,
Mud upon the ground.
No more ice on pond or river,
No more lovely snow.
Dismal rain and sloppy wetness, everywhere I go.
Please, please, Mr Weatherman,
Roll away the dark clouds, close your watering can,
Send the golden sunbeams to bring us hope and cheer,
Telling us their message: Spring will soon be here!

Nora Ward

THE RAIN

Pitter, patter, pitter, patter,
Look at all the rain,
Knocking on the window sill
And on the window pane.
Sounding like the pitter patter
Of little fairy feet,
Running down the garden path,
Running down the street.
Washing everybody's house
And everybody's shop.
Pitter patter, pitter patter
When is it going to stop?

Together with pictorial actions and voices, this verse was one of the children's favourites. All my life, outdoors has generally been preferable to indoors, in family and teaching: gardening, long hikes and picnics in all weathers. Dressed appropriately, one happily plays in sunshine or squidges through mud, stumbles over brambles and shelters from the storm, squeezily together under a large bush! Such was the accompaniment to many a song and verse.

We don't notice the wet in proper clothes.

CHAPTER 4

Winter Outdoors

AS I WENT UP THE HUMBER JUMBER

As I went up the humber jumber,
Humber jumber jeenio,
There I met Sir Hoker Poker,
Carrying away Campeenio.
If I'd had my tit, my tat,
My tit, my tat, my teenio,
I'd never have let Sir Hoker Poker
Carry away Campeenio.

Children do so love to 'fox' (trick or test) adults. Done with demonstrative actions, they get into quite a beat with this. It is a real favourite.

Tit = gun.
Humber Jumber = hill
Sir Hoker Poker = fox
Campeenio = chicken

A MASTER I HAVE

A master I have
And I am his man,
Galloping dreary dun.
And he'll get a wife
As fast as he can,
With a haily-gaily
Gambo-raily
Giggling, niggling,
Galloping galloway
Draggletail,
Dreary dun.

This is a wonderful rhyme for enunciation. You can start very slowly until your child or children know it, then gradually increase the speed until the little tongue can't keep up anymore! It is really best done while galloping about, either at home or if in class in a ring or, more fun, just about the room at random. They may get in a bit of a muddle but you can say before you begin that they must be careful of each other so you can have fun. Teachers will know best how to approach this!

Adam, He Had Seven Sons

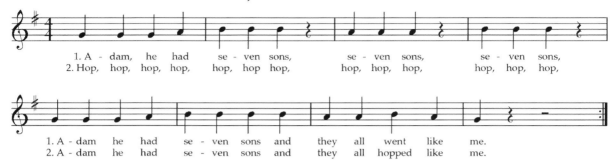

1. A - dam, he had se - ven sons, se - ven sons, se - ven sons,
2. Hop, hop, hop, hop, hop, hop hop, hop, hop, hop, hop, hop, hop,

1. A - dam he had se - ven sons and they all went like me.
2. A - dam he had se - ven sons and they all hopped like me.

Make variations as you and your children like: Jump, twizzle, flop, fly...

From Wibbleton to Wobbleton

Note: this is a pentatonic tune so it doesn't need an F sharp.

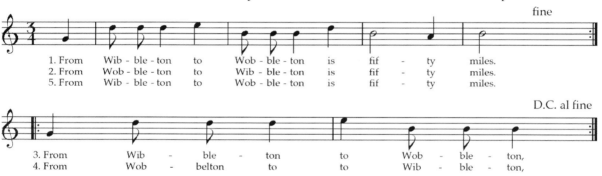

fine

1. From Wib - ble - ton to Wob - ble - ton is fif - ty miles.
2. From Wob - ble - ton to Wib - ble - ton is fif - ty miles.
5. From Wib - ble - ton to Wob - ble - ton is fif - ty miles.

D.C. al fine

3. From Wib - ble - ton to Wob - ble - ton,
4. From Wob - belton to to Wib - ble - ton,

Where are we off to?

The leader here is my son Mark at Cefn Mawr School, Wales, who helped me so much with the music in my collections.

Children walk behind each other with an adult in front, indoors or out. At the end of the song, another adult or capable child at the other end turns and leads in the opposite direction, repeating the song as long as you want, and so on until you are all tired! It can become quite exciting with a bit of imagination on the part of the leaders, varying the direction and speed. You can have the children on a rope if in a tricky place by a road, as here. There is another adult at the end, out of the picture! You can of course play it in the family. Children over about 6 can do it on their own and make it pretty exciting!!!

Italian moon

Hey Diddle, Diddle

Hey, did-dle, did-dle, the   cat and the fid-dle, the   cow   jumped o-ver the   moon.   The

lit-tle dog laughed to   see - such fun, and the   dish ran a-way with the   spoon.

Children love nonsense, yet this, as many old rhymes, has an historical origin.

OLD JOHN MUDDLECOMBE

Old John Muddlecombe has lost his cap.
He couldn't find it anywhere, the poor old chap.
He walked down the High Street and everybody said:
Silly John Muddlecombe, you've got it on your head!

Children enjoy saying this while wandering about.

59

Many years ago, I was about to leave on holiday with my children, and couldn't find the bunch of keys anywhere, generally becoming frantic. At that time, we had other buildings to lock up as well as the house. Suddenly I relaxed, stood still and quiet in a big storeroom full of muddle and 'asked' St Anthony, patron saint of lost things, to help. When I looked up, there they were in front of me on a shelf.

FEET

Big feet,
Black feet,
Going up and down the street;
Dull and shiny
Father's feet
Walk by me!

Nice feet
Brown feet
Going up and down the street;
Pretty, dainty,
Ladies' feet
Trip by me!

Small feet
Light feet
Going up and down the street;
Little children's
Happy feet
Run by me!

Irene Thompson

CRADLED COSILY

Cradled cosily, cradled deep,
Down in the warm earth baby seeds sleep.
Sleep till the spring sun climbing the skies
Shines through the darkness and bids you arise.

I Know a Little Pussy

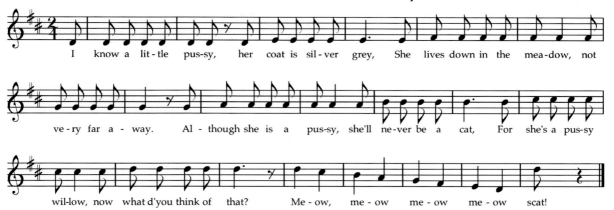

I know a lit-tle pus-sy, her coat is sil-ver grey, She lives down in the mea-dow, not ve-ry far a-way. Al-though she is a pus-sy, she'll ne-ver be a cat, For she's a pus-sy wil-low, now what d'you think of that? Me-ow, me-ow me-ow me-ow scat!

Winter scene with pussy willow catkins and snowdrops

DEEP SLEEPS THE WINTER

Deep sleeps the winter, cold, wet and grey,
Surely all the world is dead, spring is far away.
But wait, the world shall waken, it is not dead, for lo,
The fair maids of February stand in a row.

CANDLEMAS

If Candlemas be bright and clear,
There'll be two winters in one year.

LAST NIGHT

Last night before I went to bed
The moon was shining bright.
I strolled around with brother Tom
And saw a pretty sight.
It was a rabbit, bad and bad –
He came, you know, to steal.
We saw him nibble cabbage leaves
And make a hearty meal.
I s'pose we should have shooed him off
But it was quaint to see
The little fellow sitting up,
Just like a child at tea.

From an child's old picture book.

Hungry robin

Ptichka

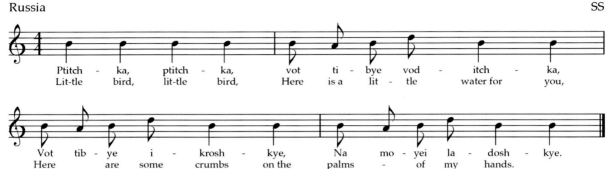

Ptitch - ka, ptitch - ka, vot ti - bye vod - itch - ka,
Lit-tle bird, lit-tle bird, Here is a lit - tle water for you,

Vot tib - ye i - krosh - kye, Na mo - yei la - dosh - kye.
Here are some crumbs on the palms - of my hands.

ПТИЧКА, LITTLE BIRD

Птичка, птичка, вот тебе водичка,
Вот тебе икрошки, на моей ладошке.

Ptichka, ptichka, vot tibye vodichka,
Vot tibye ikroshki, na moyei ladoshkye.

Little bird, Little bird, here is a little water for you,
Here are some crumbs for you on the palms of my hands.

Children particularly love this one: it speaks to the heart. We sang it in Russian but I did not translate: simply told the children what it was about. They were touched and wanted to help the hungry, thirsty little bird. It becomes clear with appropriate actions. You can of course do it in my English translation! We also sang it at Christmas.

IN THE HEART OF A SEED

In the heart of a seed, buried so deep,
A dear little plant lay fast asleep.
Wake, said the sun, and creep to the light,
Wake, said the voice of the raindrops bright.
The little plant heard, and arose to see,
What the wonderful world outside might be.

Chairs to Mend

Round for 3 voices

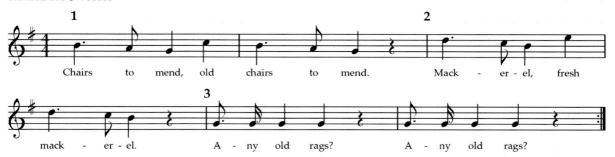

Chairs to mend, old chairs to mend. Mack - er - el, fresh
mack - er - el. A - ny old rags? A - ny old rags?

This simple song is also a round, which children enjoy as they walk about, as a man of all trades would have done with his cart in times past.

Occasionally in kindergarten, when tidying up after playtime was taking rather a long time, I began to sing this. It worked like magic, a bit like a sea shanty.

Allygaloo

Scotland

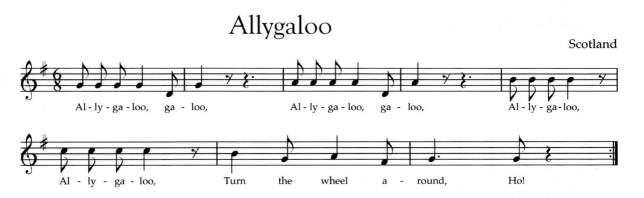

Al - ly - ga - loo, ga - loo, Al - ly - ga - loo, ga - loo, Al - ly - ga - loo,
Al - ly - ga - loo, Turn the wheel a - round, Ho!

Ring game:
Dance in a ring, jump up at ho! and dance back in the opposite direction.
This is better for children of 5 and over, as little ones can get confused.

Sunset from my house

Have You Ever Heard of the Seven League Boots?

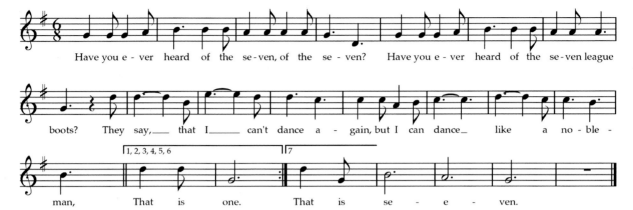

Have you e - ver heard of the se-ven, of the se - ven? Have you e - ver heard of the se-ven league boots? They say,___ that I___ can't dance a - gain, but I can dance_ like a no - ble - man, That is one. That is se - e - ven.

1. Have you ever heard of the seven, of the seven ... league boots?
Circle round
They say that I can't dance ... nobleman,
Individual circles
That is one.
Stretch one foot out.
2. *Repeat the verse, increasing by one each time at the repeat:*
That is one *Stretch one foot out.* That is two *Stretch the other foot out.*
3. That is one... *one foot.* That is two *other foot* ...That is three *kneel on one knee*
4. ... Four *kneel on the other knee*
5. ... Five *put elbow onto the floor*
6. ... Six *put the other elbow onto the floor* By this time you are getting quite out of breath!
Try stopping and say 'I am too tired, I can't go on, it's too far', etc. The children will
say 'No, we're not!' etc. Hesitate, then do the last verse very fast!
7. ... Seven *put head onto the floor!*

The following two simple rounds are loved by even quite little children. They have a
tranquil quality and can be sung on their own as a bedtime song or in class or by older
children or adults as a round. I used to sing rounds with the parents of my class for fun and
as preparation for whichever forthcoming festival; beautiful for the children. Everyone can
join in without feeling embarrassed, even if they think they 'can't sing'.

Down to the Baker's Shop

Scottish rhyme

fine

D.C. al fine

Down to the ba-ker's shop, Hop, hop, hop! My mo-ther said, to buy a loaf of bread.

HERE IS THE CHURCH

Here is the church
And here is the steeple,
Open the doors
And let out the people.

Here is the parson
Going upstairs.
And here he is
Saying his prayers.

Bell ringing

Mark, my co-music-writer for these collections, learning to ring the bells in Aldeburgh church.

Such glorious church bell ringing is an art requiring great skill and training: mathematically complicated, sociable, and unique to Great Britain.

Here is the church - *Fold second, third and fourth fingers into each other pointing downwards, so as to leave a 'flat' surface while the little fingers stand up in a triangle as the end of the church and thumbs stand up parallel to each other for the doors.*
And here is the steeple - *Now point the index fingers upwards.*
Open the doors - *Pull thumbs apart.*
And let out the people - *Turn hands inwards and upwards and wiggle fingers.*

Here is the parson - *Cross wrists and put hands back to back.*
Going upstairs. This bit is tricky! - *Stretching your arms out, put your fingers two by two between each other, starting with the little fingers until you get to the index fingers.*
And here he is - *Keeping fingers locked into each other as much as you can (I can't quite) turn your hands inwards...*
Saying his prayers - *and let one thumb wiggle out between the thumb and index finger.*

GLING, GLING, GLING, LUEG D'POESCHTLI ISCH DA
RING, RING, RING, LOOK THE POSTMAN IS HERE

I came across this delightful game in a Swiss kindergarten after I started this book. It is such a good one I feel bound to include it, although it was not among the verses and games done with children in my care. A translation is below: you will feel free to do it in your own way.

A 'postman' goes in his (invisible) van round a circle of children sitting on chairs, tapping on the shoulder of about half of them at random, who then 'step' into his post van and follow him or her in a line. The rest are 'people'.

Gling, gling, gling, lueg d'Poeschtli isch da.
Ring, ring, ring, look the postman is here.
Gling, gling, gling, vo Afrika.
Ring, ring, ring, from Africa.
Gling, gling, gling, und no en Schritt.
Ring, ring, ring, and one more step.
Gling, gling, gling, im naechschte Hus
Ring, ring, ring, in the next house
Stieget alli Paeckli uss.
All the 'parcels' climb out.
They join to a circle and sit down.

Postman goes to the 'people' still sitting, one at a time, until all have had a turn.

Grüezi Herr Poeschtler. Haend Sie es Paeckli für mich?
Hello Mr Postman, do you have a parcel for me?
Mues grad no luege.
I must just have a look.
'Postman' looks at the labels in the back of the neck of several children's clothes.
Nei, nei, nei, nei ...
No, no, no, no,
He stops at one child.
Ja, das isch es.
Yes, that's it.
Was haet's da drin?
What's in it?

The 'person' then has to say three different related things, e.g. apple, pear and orange, or aeroplane, taxi, ship. For some children this would be too advanced: they could just say one thing they like.

Rat, Tat, Tat

Rat, tat, tat, Here comes the post-man, Rat, tat, tat, with a let-ter for you.

I went down the road to post my letter. A little girl was standing by the letter box. 'It's <u>our</u> letter box,' said the little girl standing next to it. 'I see,' I said. 'May I use it?' She sighed. 'Everyone does.'

I Sent a Letter to My Love

I sent a let-ter to my love, and on the way - I dropped it, And some-one must have picked it up And put it in - his poc - ket. I dropped it, I dropped it, A - dree, a dree, I dropped it.

Children sit in a circle on the floor; one holds the 'letter' (a handkerchief), skips round outside the ring and drops it behind someone. This child jumps up and chases the other, trying to catch him or her before getting 'home', in which case the original child would have to go again; otherwise it is the turn of the new child. This game produces much excitement.

It is particularly for Valentine's Day or a party but can be played at any time of course.

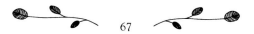

KNEE RIDES are great favourites, from babies upwards...

A FARMER WENT TROTTING

A farmer went trotting upon his grey mare,
Bumpety, bumpety, bump,
With his daughter behind him so rosy and fair,
Lumpety, lumpety lump.
A magpie called 'caw' and they all tumbled down,
Bumpety, bumpety, bump.

The mare broke her knees and the farmer his crown,
Lumpety, lumpety lump.
The mischievous magpie flew laughing away,
Bumpety, bumpety, bump,
And vowed he would serve them the same the next day.
Lumpety, lumpety lump.

Ready for a knee ride

One might think this is not very kind. However, children don't see it as the words describe, about people hurting each other. They just enjoy being wobbled about on one's knees! Many classic knee rides all over the world have such bouncy themes: that is their nature.

ANNA MARIA

Anna Maria, she sat on the fire:
(Mar-ri-a to rhyme with fire)
The fire was too hot, she sat on the pot:
The pot was too round, she sat on the ground:
The ground was too flat, she sat on the cat:*
The cat ran away with Maria on her back.

You could do this as a hand game, an action poem or knee ride.

* All such rhymes are not to be taken literally. Our adult thinking may get in the way of how children see such things: for them it is just a game and not an incentive to sit on a real cat!

FATHER AND MOTHER
AND UNCLE JOHN

Father and mother and Uncle John
Went to market, one by one.
Father fell off,
Mother fell off,
But Uncle John went on, and on,
and on, and on, and on...

As long as you want! It is exciting to do pauses between the 'and on's', varying the length of the pauses, becoming ever more thrilling!

To make this lovely toy, know that it will take you ages but think of the excitement and happiness you will bring to the recipient/s in the end.

Knit rectangles in stripes, using up bits of wool. For the kittens, stitch together at the corners in V shapes for the feet, joining in the middle, while stuffing with sheepswool.

Pull a head together out of the body, push some wool into it and sew a piece of wool round it firmly. Pull little ears out of the head and stitch. Chain crochet a short tail.

Knitted cat and kittens

For the mother cat, the same applies for the feet. The head is a separate rectangle, folded in half, stuffed well and stitched onto the head. For the tail, crochet a long chain, then work backwards and forwards in decreasing amounts to make it ever wider/narrower. Stuff as far as it will go and stitch together.

To make the 'womb' out of which the kittens can be born and unborn, make a pocket of velvet as long and wide as the body, with a zip along one side. Join it to the inside of the body seam, stuffing around it with sheepswool, so the zip can be undone and the kittens slip out and in. This plaything will keep childen quiet for a long time.

If you are near sheep, you can collect wool lying about or from a barbed wire or other fence. Pull out the bits of grass and twigs, wash and dry it well. Otherwise ask a sheep farmer or buy from a craft shop. Kapok will do if you have no sheepswool.

HOW GO LORDS AND GENTLEMEN?

How go lords and gentlemen?
Trit, trot, trit and home again.
How go the ladies, how go they?
Trit, trot, trit, trot all the way.
How goes the farmer, how goes he?
Hobble-de-gee, hobble-de-gee.
How goes the butcher's boy
Who longs to be rich?
A-gallop, a-gallop
A-plonk in the ditch.

SEE SAW SACRA DOWN

See saw sacra down,
Which is the way to London Town?
One foot up and one foot down,
That is the way to London town.

This could be a knee ride or an action poem

UNDER AND OVER

Under and Over
The dog went to Dover
When he came to the stile,
Whoops! he jumped over.

Under and Over
The dog went to Dover
When he came to the bridge,
He r-a-a-a-a-n over!

North Warren RSPB reserve, Suffolk

Little children can't get enough of this. Put baby on your lap and take the little legs in your hands, crossing them back and forth in time to the words: Under and Over, the Dog went to Dover etc. At 'Whoops!' Lift the child up. At 'the bridge', make the little legs 'run'. An extremely intelligent, elderly university professor of psychology taught me this for my children. She was lovely and great fun!

TO MARKET

To market, to market, to buy a fat pig,
Home again, home again, jiggetty jig.

To market, to market, to buy a fat hog,
Home again, home again, jiggetty jog.

Going to market

Many people will remember funny names they gave things when young and will have or know children who do. We called the marks on finger tips when immersed in water 'pig snores'. Windscreevers, waster-paster-basket, helioctober were some of my children's.

It is a wonderful thing for children to be in touch with old people, especially those who live alone and in winter, when they are less able to go out, or are not even able to go out at all. There is a growing number of early years' settings which pay regular visits to homes for old people, or who arrange transport for the elderly to the nursery or school itself. They can sing and have tea together and enjoy each others' company. Those with dementia can have a good time too. There is something that reaches across the different consciousnesses of age. Such visits kindle respect in the children for people at the other end of life's spectrum, all of whom have a rich panoply of stories to tell from a long and full life.

I lived my first four years in a converted mill in Snape, Suffolk, which was opposite the village shop and at the top of the hill. One day, having learnt to crawl (the stage so familiar to parents, when nothing is safe) I somehow escaped without anyone noticing and crawled across the drive, under the gate and into the road. The elderly shopkeeper saw me, and came out of the shop. He was physically disabled, and unable to pick me up. There were not many cars about in those days, but it so happened that at that moment one was coming up the hill. This brave man stood in the middle of the road and waved his arms about to stop the car. He thereby saved my life, enabling me to offer you, dear reader, this collection of treasures I have gathered over all these years.

APPENDIX

1. POSSIBLE ACTIONS OF MANY TO INCORPORATE INTO VERSES AND SONGS

Children enjoy a moment of suspense: a pause, a tiny antidote to the get-everything-now-rush-rush culture of today! For example, in the rhyme 'Five Fat Peas' (Summer Songbook) you can hold the child or group absolutely still for many seconds while you wait for 'popped!' I have written in the Introduction about how such verses offer natural ways for getting children to calm down and have a moment's breather. Oh, you can have so much fun with children.

Circle of children

– moves forward and back.

– goes round: I find children under 6 prefer to go always the same way rather than changing about, which tends to confuse them. Clockwise seems natural. The exceptions are the maypole and making a spiral.

– lays hands on each others' shoulders, sitting or standing. I created this for a picture of inclusiveness and love for each other.

– makes a spiral: walking round once left, then an adult stands still and lets go of the right hand person (adult or capable child of 6 or over) who continues to walk round. This becomes a spiral, and it can become rather squashy in the middle but children enjoy that. The second adult/child then walks back round sideways to return to make a circle. Over 6 or 7, children are able to follow without holding hands.

– holding hands, children lift arms up to make windows or doors. Some other games also require hand-holding; there are children who don't like touching. If the game is tricky without, holding a snippet of the neighbour's T-shirt or pullover works just fine, or even just keeping close.

An easy way to get children to come together in a ring in the setting or even at a party without telling them to is to take the hands of a couple and sing:

'Here we come together': Move into the centre of the space, sing a simple scale up: CDEFG, then 'And here we go again': move back, singing down GFEDC. Repeat.

This movement and song catch their interest so they probably gradually join in. In a class, once they have done it on a few days, they will likely come when you hold out your hands at the appropriate time without saying anything. It is magical what you can achieve: moving or gesturing silently in some way suits the consciousness of the young child.

It is very nice to end a circle session with a few moments of stillness, standing or sitting.

Individual movements

Little or big circles, wandering about, running, swirling outwards and returning

Large – medium – small

Up – down, in – out, fast – slow, especially a combination of contrasting ones

Heels – toes – fingers – palms – fingertips – fists – wrists – elbows – knees – head

Stand – kneel – bend – sit – lie down – crawl – leap – jump – hop – skip – stamp – roll – trot – wriggle (also fingers and toes) – tip toe – on one leg

Jump up and down, or also forward; for some games together with clapping, joyful!

Open and close hands, toes or feet, crouch, squeeze into a little ball

Climb over or through something real or imaginary or each other

Balance on one leg or walk across a bridge or plank, likewise real or imaginary

Make waves, butterflies or swim with thumbs crossed, hands flat

Strong – floppy, wobbly – straight: make funny movements with feet, arms or hands:

Fold arms around oneself, or arms make a cradle

Cupping hands at the waist or in front for a reverent gesture

A pleading or reverent movement forwards, one hand a little in front of the other

Put hands together, outer sides together to make a larger 'cup'

Gentle swaying sideways or forwards and backwards e.g. for a tree

Walk backwards

Animal movements, e.g. nibbling, hunching up or making a tail

Run hands or fingers up and down hands, arms or round about body

Sounds

Loud – soft, Sweet – croaky, High – low, Fast – slow, Squeaky – gruff

Mouth (small motor skills): whistle, yawn, teeth chattering, teeth grinding (the mill!), tongue quickly in and out on top lip, pouting

Clapping – tapping – knocking

Sometimes in a circle time that involved going 'somewhere else', we went right out of the room, sometimes *even outside*, singing away and doing the actions to match the song as we went. Children really loved that, it was *really* exciting, even if they went in and out normally several times a day. I never said I would, we just did! We wore slippers indoors so I only went onto clean, hard surfaces, but always the same, the same, every time. Occasionally we squeezed into a tiny space in or outdoors: in autumn it was my big walk-in cupboard with a relevant song and a little safety glass lantern where it was dark, squashed together with myself holding the odd timid child close. Other times it was a big dark bush 'sheltered' from the rain, or a shed. This was a wonderful, strengthening experience some of those children still speak of today. It helped some overcome their fear of the dark. I believe it is worth going beyond boundaries for good and sensibly safe reasons.

Everything above is not everything by a long chalk! Let your imagination fly!

2. RHYMING WORDS

Over the years I compiled this list for students to encourage them to make their own verses. You can find such lists on the internet now. However, you may find this paper version quite handy. Many words can of course have an 's' at the end for a plural or verb.

And	Along	Beat	Found	Agree	Absurd
Band	Bong	Eat	Ground	Bee	Bird
Fanned	Dong	Feet	Hound	Free	Curd
Grand	Long	Fleet	Mound	He	Heard
Hand	Song	Heat	Pound	Key	Third
Land	Wrong	Meat	Round	Knee	Word
Planned	(On)	Meet	Sound	Lee	
Sand		Neat		Me	Dawn
Stand	Stop	Pete	Benign	Plea	Fawn
	Top	Seat	Brine	Sea	Forlorn
Blow	Knock	Sheet	Divine	See	Form
Bow	Clock	Treat	Fine	She	Morn
Crow	Sock		Line	Tea	Pawn
Doe	Hop	Keep	Mine	Three	Shorn
Foe	Pop	Leap	Nine	Tree	Torn
Glow	Plop	Neap	Pine		
Grow	Cock	Seep	Sign	Agrees	Moon
Hoe		Sleep	Whine	Bees	Soon
Low	Byre	Weep	Grime	Breeze	Tune
Mow	Crier		Mime	Frees	
Row	Fire	Ate	Rhyme	Freeze	Bow
Sew	Higher	Bait		He's	How
So	Lyre	Date	Haste	Keys	Now
Toe	Mire	Eight	Paste	Knees	Sow
	Pyre	Fate	Taste	Pleas	Trow
Ding	Spire	Great	Waste	Please	Vow
Fling	Tire	Hate		Seas	
King	Wire	Late	Alone	Sees	Begun
Ring		Mate	Crone	She's	Done
Sing		Wait	Flown	Sneeze	Fun
Spring			Groan	Teas	One
Sting		Dish	Lone	Tease	Run
String		Fish	Moan	Trees	Son
Ting		Swish	Phone		Spun
Wing		Wish	Stone		Sun
Wring			Home		Ton
And verbs			Loam		Won
ending in –ing					

Funny	Today	Bright	Deal
Honey	Tray	Fight	Feel
Money	Way	Fright	Heal
Mummy	Yea	Light	Heel
Runny		Night	Meal
Sunny	Dear	Right	Peal
Tummy	Deer	Sight	Peel
	Ear	Slight	Seal
Bung	Fear	Tight	Steal
Hung	Here	Height	Zeal
Rung	Rear	Kite	
Sung	Sear	Might	Buy
Wrung	Tear	Mite	By
		Site	Die
Blew	Air	White	Dye
Blue	Bare		Fly
Dew	Bear	Dove	Fry
Do	Bear (to carry)	Love	High
Few	Dare	Shove	Lie
Hew	Fair	Above	My
Hue	Fare		Nigh
Moo	Hair	Caw	Pry
New	Hare	Core	Sigh
Through	Lair	Door	Tie
Too	Mare	For	Try
True	Stair	Haw	Why
Two	Stare	Implore	
You	Tare	Lore	Face
Zoo	Tear	More	Grace
	Where	Nor	Lace
Bay		Paw	Pace
Day	Afar	Poor	Case
Grey	Ajar	Raw	Chase
Hay	Bar	Saw	
Hooray	Car	Shore	
Lay	Far	Sore	
May	Mar	Sure	
Nay	Star	Tore	
Pay	Tar	Wore	
Play		Your	
Say			
Stay			

3. AN EXAMPLE OF A WINTER CIRCLE TIME SEQUENCE

Many readers will be used to creating a circle time. Maybe what follows could help others. I called mine 'ringtime' as I prefer its sound. Verses of a more general nature can supplement seasonal ones. Although you use songs and rhymes again and again, you may not want to repeat a sequence. Some settings have children of one age; others across two or more years, so the length varies accordingly.

You may like a little phrase leading from one item to another; I preferred a gesture or gestures from the following piece. You can of course use a whole story (or make one up), maybe with repetitions, which leads naturally from one verse to another. Although I believe it is better not to be dramatic with young children, you can be gently dramatic by varying the sounds you make.

Below is an example of a winter ringtime (verses taken from this book) for a mixed age group, using variety, flow from one item to the other, the whole circle moving, individual actions, large and fine motor skills, sitting, standing or kneeling, different moods, sung or recited. Each item would be repeated at least three times. It might take around 20 minutes. My experience is that a varied, lively circle time for a mixed age group will hold the children for up to half an hour, or a little fairytale play, some of which I hope to publish soon. New children don't always want to join in, but later they may do if taken by interesting sounds and movements! You will shorten it for a younger group of course; for a parent and child group, 1. 2. 3. 4. 5. 12. would be enough, with lots of repetition for little ones!

It has always been irrelevant whether we have had snow or not. If it does come, even a few flakes are exciting. For many children it is the norm; for others a fairy tale.

1. Bye Baby Bunting

1. Sung, gentle action rhyme.

2. I can tie my shoelaces, I can brush my hair

2. Sitting or standing, action rhyme, small motor skills.

3. Bubble, said the kettle, bubble, said the pot

4. Mrs Mason broke a basin

5. Five fat sausages

3.4.5. Standing or sitting, action or finger rhymes, large and/or small motor skills.

Children love funny poems with funny actions.

6. Down to the baker's shop, hop, hop, hop

6. Action song, moving in a circle or about the room, large motor skills.

7. Have you ever heard of the seven, of the seven

7. Circle action rhyme, standing, kneeling, makes breathless!

8. Look out, look out, Jack Frost is about

8. Action poem, quick movements in a circle or freely about the room.

9. Oh where do you come from, you little flakes of snow

10. The snowflakes are whirling so fast and so light

11. The North wind doth blow

12. Up among the branches, not so very high

9.10.11.12. One spoken, three sung action poems, standing or sitting

13. Ptichka, ptichka, Little bird

13. Sung, gentle action rhyme. You could do it in couples as bird and child.

This reverent little song makes a lovely way to end the ring.

4. SEASONAL STORIES

Although one can tell a story at any time, I tended to relate many to the time of the year: the season in nature or inner belief (in my case Christianity; you would want to relate them to your own if different). For example, those with a theme of renewal or transformation I found particularly suitable for spring and Easter. In summer, when the days are long and people enjoy parties outdoors, I would tell stories with a silly, forgetful or arrogant theme, which often have a theme of particular consciousness alongside: for example 'The Three Sillies' (English Fairy Tales) or 'King Thrushbeard' (Grimm).

In autumn there would be tales of courage as the days grow shorter and darkness descends upon the earth. At Advent (the four weeks leading up to Christmas) I liked to tell stories of giving and kindness, and at Christmas those of newness and joy. In winter, when we seek warmth and tend to stay indoors, one can use stories with a theme of sleepiness and not paying attention, like 'Mashenka and the Bear' (Russian fairytale).

I related all my teaching work to the time of the year. This makes sense to children; they build on their knowledge and respond well, while enjoying remembering how it was last year, 'when I was only little'. You may like to do the same for your own family.

Fairytales are to be found all over the world in a multitude of tongues with the same underlying themes. I have listed here some of those which are easy to find. *English Fairy Tales* is the collection of Joseph Jacobs. The Routledge edtition of *Grimms Fairy Tales* tells them as they should be, with the gruesomeness and redemption so often left out in sweetened versions and picture books but which to my mind are an essential point of those particular stories. Children like to know that things turn out all right and that the baddy gets his or her just deserts. It is important though that one tells them rather deadpan to children under seven or eight, without emotion, for that is when they would become frightening. Also it allows children to make their own inner pictures, which is not possible on screen. I actually learnt mine by heart so the children were free to make their own images, but when I had a beautiful picture book with the proper story and without caricatures, I would use that. There are a few stories listed below in other books not hard to find.

The numbers to the right refer to the age from which I find them suitable.
Seven-Year-Old WB denotes *The Seven-Year-Old Wonder Book* by Isabel Wyatt.

I cannot list the best stories of all: your own or 'When Uncle John was little...'

Epiphany

La Befana

(a wonderful Italian tale which you can find in brief on Wikipedia, but perhaps you know an Italian who can tell you the story) 4

The Shepherd Boy's Flute Dan Lindholm 4

(out of print but worth looking for)

Winter

The Town Musicians of Bremen	Grimm	4
The Brave Little Tailor	Grimm	5
The Tomten (wonderful picture book)	Astrid Lindgren	3
The Fox and the Tomten (ditto)	Astrid Lindgren	3
Fundevogel	Grimm	4
The Giant and the Tailor	Grimm	5
The Golden Key	Grimm	4
The Goose Girl at the Well	Grimm	5
Hansel and Gretel	Grimm	5
How the Snow got its Colour	Dan Lindholm	3

(out of print but worth looking for)

The Hut in the Forest	Grimm	6
Little Red Cap (Red Riding Hood)	Grimm	4
Maschenka and the Bear		4

(Russian fairy tale, also in the Autumn collection but good in winter too)

The Nixie of the Mill Pond	Grimm	6
The Old Man's Mitten		2

(wonderful Ukrainian story to be found in various books)

Old Rink Rank	Grimm	5
The Pied Piper of Hamelin		6
Rapunzel	Grimm	5
Saint Joseph in the Wood	Grimm	5
Scrapefoot	English Fairy Tales	3
Sweet Porridge	English Fairy Tales	3
The Three Bears		2
The Three Little Men in the Wood	Grimm	5

(one of my favourite tales)

The Three Wishes	English Fairy Tales	4
The Twelve Dancing Princesses	Grimm	4

(As with many fairy tales, there are various picture books and DVDs of this beautiful tale, yet you may prefer just to read or tell the story and let your children make their own inner pictures.)

The Wolf and the Seven Little Kids	Grimm	3

Where did I hear, '*Logic gets you from A to B. Imagination gets you anywhere. Imagination is the most precious of all our possessions*'? Perhaps one could add to this 'Inspiration' and also 'Intuition' in equal measure.

It is fun to see what one can achieve when using one or all of these while entering into the young child's world. For example, in kindergarten we might all be sitting, ready for me to tell the story, whilst I knew that some clothes and shoes were not put away very tidily after playing outside. I might say: 'There's a lot of noise in the cloakroom… I can't tell the story with all that going on…' and the children might look round and respond with 'It's the boots playing up,' and run out to sort everything out. Or I would begin: 'Once upon a time, a long, long time ago, when was it, when indeed was it not, there lived an old…'. Here I might stop and listen acutely. The children, surprised at this interruption, would listen too. 'It's the coat's crying,' I might say. A child might say: 'I know, the coats are upset because they are in a mess!' And off they would go to sort them out, returning contentedly for the story when all was well again. A happy opportunity for the children to do it without instruction! With a sigh of contentment I would begin again. 'Once upon a time…'

It is nice to praise a child under about 7 indirectly. For example 'Your shoes are so smiley!' when they were put away neatly, and the child would glow.

On a visit to a local primary school where I made music with all the children, there was a child of 8 in his wheelchair who could barely move nor speak nor make any noise. When I played on my harp he beamed one of the greatest 'sunshines' I have ever seen in a child. His carer held his hand and shook some bells with him. Then I pulled the harp to him, held his hand and plucked some strings with him. He was oozing silent rapture. Then I let go his hand: he kept it there and plucked the strings *on his own*. I found it hard to keep back the tears at this magical experience. I am gently weeping from the memory as I write. He lit up the whole hall with joy.

Music encompasses all learning and should be central to every child's education.

SOURCES

The Book of a Thousand Poems, Evans Brothers Ltd
The Clarendon Singing Games, Books 1 and 2, Oxford University Press
The Oxford Dictionary of Nursery Rhymes, Iona and Peter Opie, Oxford University Press
The Oxford Book of Children's Verse, Iona and Peter Opie, Oxford University Press
The Puffin Book of Nursery Rhymes, Iona and Peter Opie, Puffin Books
This Little Puffin, compiled by Elizabeth Matterson, Puffin Books
A Puffin Book of Verse, compiled by Eleanor Graham, Puffin Books
The Oxford Book of Carols, Oxford University Press

Further reading:
Well, I Wonder, Childhood in the Modern World, A Handbook for Parents, Teachers and Carers, Sally Schweizer, Sophia Books
Under the Sky, Playing, Working and Enjoying Adventures in the Open Air, A Handbook for Parents, Teachers and Carers, Sally Schweizer, Sophia Books
My Brother Benjamin, Beth Britten, Faber Finds, edited by Sally Schweizer

Britten family 1914. l-r: Beth, mother Edith, Benjamin, Barbara, Robert.

Online resources can be found on my 'Sally Schweizer' YouTube channel
or on my blog at sallyschweizer.blogspot.co.uk

INDEX OF FIRST LINES
(*songs are in italics*)